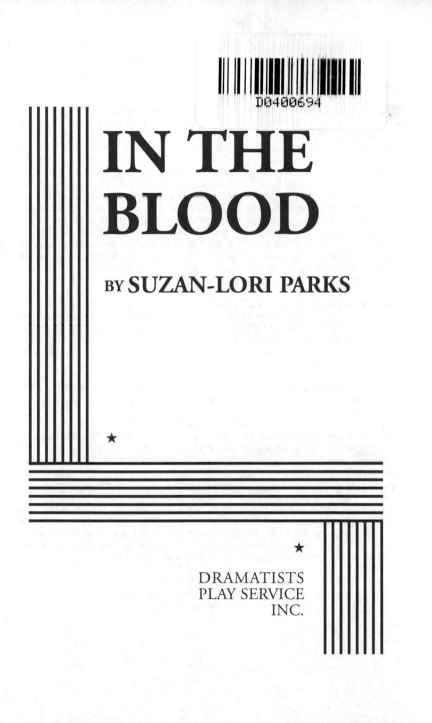

IN THE BLOOD

BY SUZAN-LORI PARKS

DRAMATISTS
PLAY SERVICE
INC.

IN THE BLOOD
Copyright © 2000, Suzan-Lori Parks

All Rights Reserved

Original New York Production by
The New York Shakespeare Festival,
George C. Wolfe, Producer

IN THE BLOOD premiered at The Joseph Papp Public Theatre/New York Shakespeare Festival (George C. Wolfe, Producer; Rosemarie Tichler, Artistic Producer; Mark Litvin, Managing Director) in New York City in November 1999. It was directed by David Esbjornson; the set design was by Narelle Sissons; the lighting design was by Jane Cox; the sound design was by Don DiNicola; the costume design was by Elizabeth Hope Clancy; the production dramaturg was John Dias; and the production stage manager was Kristen Harris. The cast was as follows:

HESTER, LA NEGRITA .... Charlayne Woodard
CHILLI/JABBER .... Rob Campbell
REVEREND D./BABY .... Reggie Montgomery
THE WELFARE LADY/BULLY .... Gail Grate
THE DOCTOR/TROUBLE .... Bruce MacVittie
AMIGA GRINGA/BEAUTY .... Deirdre O'Connell

AUTHOR'S NOTES

This play requires a cast of six adult actors, five of whom double as adults and children. The setting should be spare, to reflect the poverty of the world of the play.

I'm continuing the use of my slightly unconventional theatrical elements. Here's a road map.

(Rest.)
Take a little time, a pause, a breather; make a transition.

A Spell
An elongated and heightened *(Rest.)*. Denoted by repetition of figures' names with no dialogue. Has sort of an architectural look:

REVEREND D.
HESTER.
REVEREND D.
HESTER.

This is a place where the figures experience their pure true simple state. While no action or stage business is necessary, directors should fill this moment as they best see fit.

[Brackets in the text indicate optional cuts for production.]

(Parentheses around dialogue indicate softly spoken passages (asides; sotto voce).)

CHARACTERS

Hester, La Negrita
Chilli/Jabber, her oldest son
Reverend D./Baby, her youngest son
The Welfare Lady/Bully, her oldest daughter
The Doctor/Trouble, her middle son
Amiga Gringa/Beauty, her youngest daughter

PLACE

Here

TIME

Now

IN THE BLOOD

SCENE 1
UNDER THE BRIDGE

Home under the bridge. The word "SLUT" scrawled on a wall. Hesters oldest child Jabber, 13, studies that scrawl. Hester lines up soda cans as her youngest child Baby, 2 yrs old, watches.

HESTER. Zit uh good word or a bad word?

JABBER.
JABBER.

HESTER. Aint like you to have yr mouth shut, Jabber. Say it to me and we can figure out the meaning together.
JABBER. Naaaa —
HESTER. What I tell you bout saying "Naa" when you mean "no"? You talk like that people wont think you got no brains and Jabbers got brains. All my kids got brains, now.
(Rest.)
Lookie here, Baby. Mamma set the cans for you. Mamma gonna show you how to make some money. Watch.
JABBER. Im slow.
HESTER. Slow aint never stopped nothing, Jabber. You bring yr foot down on it and smash it flat. Howabout that, Baby? Put it in the pile and thats that. Now you try.
(Baby jumps on the can smashing it flat, hollering as he smashes.)
BABY. Ha!

HESTER. Yr a natural! Jabber, yr little baby brothers a natural. We gonna come out on top this month, I can feel it. Try another one, Baby.

JABBER. They wrote it in yr practice place.

HESTER. Yes they did.

JABBER. They wrote in yr practice place so you didnt practice today.

HESTER. I practiced. In my head. In the air. In the dirt underfoot.

JABBER. Lets see.

(With great difficulty Hester makes an "A" in the dirt.)

HESTER. The letter A.

JABBER. Almost.

HESTER. You gonna disparage me I aint gonna practice.

BABY. Mommmmieee!

HESTER. Gimmieuhminute, Baby-child.

JABBER. Legs apart hands crost the chest like I showd you. Try again.

BABY. Mommieee!

HESTER. See the pretty can, Baby?

BABY. Ha!

JABBER. Try again.

BABY. Mommmieee!

HESTER. Later. Read that word out to me, huh? I like it when you read to me.

JABBER. Dont wanna read it.

HESTER. Cant or wont?

JABBER. — Cant.

HESTER.
JABBER.

(He knows what the word says, but he wont say it.)

HESTER. I was sick when I was carrying you. Damn you, slow fool. Aaah, my treasure, cmmeer. My oldest treasure. *(She gives him a quick hug. Hester looks at the word, its letters mysterious to her. Baby smashes can after can.)*

Go scrub it off, then. I like my place clean.

(Jabber dutifully scrubs the wall.)

We know who writ it up there. It was them bad boys writing on my home. And in my practice place. Do they write on they own homes? I dont think so. They come under the bridge and write things they dont write nowhere else. A mean ugly word, I'll bet. A word to hurt our feelings. And because we aint lucky we gotta live with it. 5 children I got. 5 treasures. 5 joys. But we aint got our leg up, just yet. So we gotta live with mean words and hurt feelings.
JABBER. Words dont hurt my feelings, Mamma.
HESTER. Dont disagree with me.
JABBER. Sticks and stones, Mamma.
HESTER. Yeah. I guess.
(Rest.)
Too late for yr sisters and brother to still be out. Yr little brother Babys gonna make us rich. He learns quick. Look at him go.
(She lines up more cans and Baby jumps on them, smashing them all. Bully, her 12-yr-old girl, runs in.)
BULLY. Mommieeeeeeeeee! Mommie, Trouble he has really done it this time. I told him he was gonna be doing life and he laughed and then I said he was gonna get the electric chair and you know what he said?
HESTER. Help me sack the cans.
BULLY. He said a bad word!
HESTER. Sack the cans.
(They sack the crushed cans.)
BULLY. Trouble he said something really bad but Im not saying it cause if I do yll wash my mouth. What he said was bad but what he did, what he did was worse.
HESTER. Whatd he do?
BULLY. Stole something.
HESTER. Food?
BULLY. No.
HESTER. Toys?
BULLY. No.
HESTER. I dont like youall stealing toys and I dont like youall stealing food but it happens. I wont punish you for it. Yr just kids. Trouble thinks with his stomach. He hungry he takes, sees a toy, gotta have it.
BULLY. A policeman saw him steal and ran after him but Trouble

9

ran faster cause the policeman was fat.

HESTER. Policeman chased him?

BULLY. He had a big stomach. Like he was pregnant. He was jiggling and running and yelling and red in the face.

HESTER. What he steal?

BULLY. — Nothing.

HESTER. You talk that much and you better keep talking, Miss.

(Bully buttons her lips. Hester pops her upside the head.)

BULLY. Owwww!

HESTER. Get outa my sight. Worse than a thief is a snitch that dont snitch.

(Trouble, age 10 and Beauty, age 7, run in, breathless. They see Hester eyeing them and stop running; they walk nonchalantly.)

What you got behind you?

TROUBLE. Nothing. Jabber, what you doing?

JABBER. Cleaning the wall.

BEAUTY. My hair needs a ribbon.

HESTER. Not right now it dont. You steal something?

TROUBLE. Me? Whats cookin?

HESTER. Soup of the day.

TROUBLE. We had soup the day yesterday.

HESTER. Todays a new day.

BEAUTY. Is it a new soup?

HESTER. Wait and see. You gonna end up in the penitentiary and embarass your mother?

TROUBLE. No.

HESTER. If you do I'll kill you. Set the table.

JABBER. Thats girls work.

TROUBLE. Mommiee —

BULLY. Troubles doing girls work Troubles doing girls work.

HESTER. Set the damn table or Ima make a girl outa you!

TROUBLE. You cant make a girl outa me.

HESTER. Dont push me!

(Rest.)

Look, Baby. See the soup? Mommies stirring it. Dont come close, its hot.

BEAUTY. I want a ribbon.

HESTER. Get one I'll tie it in.

10

(Beauty gets a ribbon. Trouble gets bowls, wipes them clean, hands them out. Hester follows behind him and, out of the back of his pants, yanks a policemans club.)
Whered you get this?

TROUBLE.
HESTER.
TROUBLE.

HESTER. I said —
TROUBLE. I found it. On the street. It was just lying there.
BULLY. You stole it.
TROUBLE. Did not!
HESTER. Dont lie to me.
TROUBLE. I found it. I did. It was just lying on the street. I was minding my own business.
HESTER. That why the cops was chasing you?
TROUBLE. Snitch!
BULLY. Jailbait!
(Bully hits Trouble hard. They fight. Pandemonium.)
HESTER. Suppertime!
(Order is restored. Hester slips the club into the belt of her dress; it hangs there like a sword. She wears it like this for most of the play. Her children sit in a row holding their bowls. She ladles out the soup.)
Todays soup the day, ladies and gents, is a very special blend of herbs and spices. The broth is chef Mommies worldwide famous "whathaveyou" stock. Theres carrots in there. Theres meat. Theres oranges. Theres pie.
TROUBLE. What kinda pie?
HESTER. What kind you like?
TROUBLE. Apple.
HESTER. Theres apple pie.
JABBER. Pumpkin.
BULLY. And cherry!
HESTER. Theres pumpkin and cherry too. And steak. And mash potatoes for Beauty. And milk for Baby.
BEAUTY. And diamonds.
JABBER. You cant eat diamonds.

HESTER. So when you find one in yr soup whatll you do?
BEAUTY. Put it on my finger.
(They slurp down their soup quickly. As soon as she fills their bowls, theyre empty again. The kids eat. Hester doesnt.)
JABBER. You aint hungry?
HESTER. I'll eat later.
JABBER. You always eating later.
HESTER. You did a good job with the wall, Jabber. Whatd that word say anyway?
JABBER. — Nothing.
(The soup pot is empty.)

HESTER.
JABBER/BULLY/TROUBLE/BEAUTY/BABY.

(Rest.)
HESTER. Bedtime.
BULLY. Could we have a story?
(Rest.)
HESTER. All right.
(Rest.)
There were once these five brothers and they were all big and strong and handsome and didnt have a care in the world. One was known for his brains so they called him Smarts and one was known for his muscles, so they called him Toughguy, the third one was a rascal so they called him Wild, the fourth one was as goodlooking as all get out and they called him Looker and the fifth was the youngest and they called him Honeychild cause he was as young as he was sweet. And they was always together these five brothers. Everywhere they went they always went together. No matter what they was always together cause they was best friends and wasnt nothing could divide them. And there was this Princess. And she lived in a castle and she was lonesome. She was lonesome and looking for love but she couldnt leave her castle so she couldnt look very far so every day she would stick her head out her window and sing to the sun and every night she would stick her head out and sing to the moon and the stars: "Where are you?" And one day the five brothers heard her and came calling and she looked upon them and she said: "There are five

12

of you, and each one is wonderful and special in his own way. But the law of my country doesnt allow a princess to have more than one husband." And that was such bad news and they were all so in love that they all cried. Until the Princess had an idea. She was after all the Princess, so she changed the law of the land and married them all.

(Rest.)

And with Bro Smarts she had a baby named Jabber. And with Bro Toughguy she had Bully. With Bro Wild came Trouble. With Bro Looker she had Beauty. With Bro Honeychild came Baby. And they was all happy.

JABBER. Until the bad news came.

HESTER. No bad news came.

JABBER. Theres always bad news.

HESTER. Bedtime.

BEAUTY. Where did the Daddys go?

HESTER. They went to bed.

TROUBLE. They ran off.

JABBER. The war came and the brothers went off to fight and they all died.

BEAUTY. They all died?

JABBER. And they fell into the ground and the dirt covered up they heads.

HESTER. Its bedtime. Now!

BEAUTY. Im scared.

TROUBLE. I aint scared. Jabber, you a spook.

BULLY. Yr the spook.

TROUBLE. Yr a bastard.

BULLY. Yr a bastard.

HESTER. Yr all bastards!

(The children burst into tears.)

Cmmeer. Cmmeer. Mama loves you. Shes just tired is all. Lemmie hug you.

(They nestle around her and she hugs them.)

My 5 treasures. My 5 joys.

HESTER.
JABBER/BULLY/TROUBLE/BEAUTY/BABY.
HESTER.

HESTER. Lets hit the sack! And leave yr shoes for polish and yr shirts and blouses for press. You dont wanna look like you dont got nobody.
(They take off their shoes and tops and go inside leaving Hester outside alone.)

HESTER.
HESTER.
HESTER.

(Rest.)
(She examines the empty soup pot, shines the kids shoes, "presses" their clothes. A wave of pain shoots through her.)
You didnt eat, Hester. And the pain in yr gut comes from having nothing in it.
(Rest.)
Kids ate good though. Ate their soup all up. They wont starve.
(Rest.)
None of these shoes shine. Never did no matter how hard you spit on em, Hester. You get a leg up the first thing you do is get shoes. New shoes for yr 5 treasures. You got yrself a good pair of shoes already.
(From underneath a pile of junk she takes a shoebox. Inside is a pair of white pumps. She looks them over then puts them away.)
Dont know where yr going but yll look good when you get there.
[*(She takes out a small tape player. Pops in a tape. She takes a piece of chalk from her pocket and, on the freshly scrubbed wall, practices her letters: She writes the letter A over and over and over. The cassette tape plays as she writes.)*
REVEREND D. *(On tape.)* If you cant always do right then you got to admit that some times, some times my friends you are going to do wrong and you are going to have to *live* with that. Somehow work that into the fabric of your life. Because there aint a soul out there that is spot free. There aint a soul out there that has walked but hasnt stumbled. Aint a single solitary soul out there that has said "hello" and not "goodbye," has said "yes" to the lord and "yes" to the devil too, has drunk water and drunk wine, loved and hated, experienced the good side of the tracks and the bad. That is what

they call "Livin," friends. L-I-V-I-N, friends. Life on earth is full of confusion. Life on earth is full of misunderstandings, reprimandings, and we focus on the trouble, friends when it is the solution to those troubles we oughta be looking at. "I have fallen and I cant get up!" How many times have you heard that, friends? The fellow on the street with his whisky breath and his outstretched hand, the banker scraping the money off the top, the runaway child turned criminal all cry out "I have fallen, and I cant get up!" "I have fallen, and I cant get up!" "I have fallen — "

(Hester hears someone coming and turns the tape off.] She goes back to polishing the shoes. Amiga Gringa comes in.)

AMIGA GRINGA. Look at old Mother Hubbard or whatever.

HESTER. Keep quiet. Theyre sleeping.

AMIGA GRINGA. The old woman and the shoe. Thats who you are.

HESTER. I get my leg up thats what Im getting. New shoes for my treasures.

AMIGA GRINGA. Thatll be some leg up.

HESTER. You got my money?

AMIGA GRINGA. Is that a way to greet a friend? "You got my money?" What world is this?

HESTER. You got my money, Amiga?

AMIGA GRINGA. I got *news* for you, Hester. News thats better than gold. But first — heads up.

(The Doctor comes in. He wears a sandwich board and carries all his office paraphernalia on his back.)

DOCTOR. Hester! Yr due for a checkup.

HESTER. My guts been hurting me.

DOCTOR. Im on my way home just now. Catch up with me tomorrow. We'll have a look at it then.

(He goes on his way.)

AMIGA GRINGA. Doc! I am in pain like you would not believe. My hips, Doc. When I move them — blinding flashes of light and then — down I go, flat on my back, like Im dead, Doc.

DOCTOR. I gave you something for that yesterday.

DOCTOR.
AMIGA GRINGA.

(He slips Amiga a few pills. He goes on his way.)
AMIGA GRINGA. He's a saint.
HESTER. Sometimes.
AMIGA GRINGA. Want some?
HESTER. I want my money.
AMIGA GRINGA. Patience, girl. All good things are on their way. Do you know what the word is?
HESTER. What word?
AMIGA GRINGA. Word is that yr first love is back in town, doing well and looking for you.
HESTER. Chilli? Jabbers daddy? Looking for me?
AMIGA GRINGA. Thats the word.

HESTER.
HESTER.

HESTER. Bullshit. Gimmie my money, Miga. I promised the kids cake and ice cream. How much you get?
AMIGA GRINGA. First, an explanation of the economic environment.
HESTER. Just gimmie my money —
AMIGA GRINGA. The Stock Market, The Bond Market, Wall Street, Grain Futures, Bulls and Bears and Pork Bellies. They all impact the price a woman such as myself can get for a piece of "found" jewlery.
HESTER. That werent jewlery I gived you that was a watch. A Mans watch. Name brand. And it was working.
AMIGA GRINGA. Do you know what the Dow did today, Hester? The Dow was up twelve points. And that prize fighter, the one everyone is talking about, the one with the pretty wife and the heavyweight crown, he rang the opening bell. She wore a dress cut down to here. And the Dow shot up 43 points in the first minutes of trading, Hester. Up like a rocket. And men glanced up at the clocks on the walls of their offices and women around the country glanced into the faces of their children and time passed. [And someone looks at their watch because its lunchtime, Hester. And theyre having — lunch. And they wish it would last forever. Cause when they get back to their office where they — work, when they

16

get back the Dow has plummeted. And theres a lot of racing around and time is brief and something must be done before the closing bell. Phone calls are made, marriages dissolve, promises lost in the shuffle, Hester, and all this time your Amiga Gringa is going from fence to fence trying to get the best price on this piece of "found" jewelry. Numbers racing on lightboards, Hester, telling those that are in the know, the value of who knows what. One man, broken down in tears in the middle of the avenue, "oh my mutual funds" he was saying.] The market was hot, and me, a suspicious looking mother, very much like yrself, with no real address and no valid forms of identification, walking the streets with a hot watch.
(Rest.)
Here.
(She gives Hester $.)
HESTER. Wheres the rest?
AMIGA GRINGA. Thats it.
HESTER. 5 bucks?
AMIGA GRINGA. It wasnt a good day. Some days are good some days are bad. I kept a buck for myself.
HESTER. You stole from me.
AMIGA GRINGA. Dont be silly. We're friends, Hester.
HESTER. I shoulda sold it myself.
AMIGA GRINGA. But you had the baby to watch.
HESTER. And no ones gonna give money to me with me carrying Baby around. Still I coulda got more than 5.
AMIGA GRINGA. Go nextime yrself then. The dangers I incur, working with you. You oughta send yr kids away. Like me. I got 3 kids. All under the age of 3. And do you see me looking all baggy eyed, up all night shining little shoes and flattening little shirts and going without food? Theres plenty of places that you can send them. Homes. Theres plenty of peoples, rich ones especially, that cant have kids. The rich spend days looking through the newspaper for ads where they can buy one. Or they go to the bastard homes and pick one out. Youd have some freedom. Youd have a chance at life. Like me.
HESTER. My kids is mine. I get rid of em what do I got? Nothing. I got nothing now, but if they go I got less than nothing.
AMIGA GRINGA. Suit yrself. You wouldnt have to send them

all away, just one or two or three.

HESTER. All I need is a leg up. I get my leg up I'll be ok.

(Bully comes outside and stands there watching them. She wears pink, one-piece, flame-retardant pajamas.)

What.

BULLY. My hands stuck.

HESTER. Why you sleep with yr hands in fists?

AMIGA GRINGA. Yr an angry girl, arentcha, Bully.

BULLY. Idunno. This ones stuck too.

HESTER. Maybe yll grow up to be a boxer, huh? We can watch you ringside, huh? *Wide World of Sports.*

AMIGA GRINGA. Presenting in this corner weighing 82 pounds the challenger: Bully!

BULLY. Ima good girl.

HESTER. Course you are. There. You shouldnt sleep with yr hands balled up. The good fairies come by in the night with treats for little girls and they put them in yr hands. How you gonna get any treats if yr hands are all balled up?

BULLY. Jabber is bad and Trouble is bad and Beauty is bad and Baby is bad but I'm good. Bullys a good girl.

HESTER. Go on back to bed now.

BULLY. Miga. Smell.

AMIGA GRINGA. You got bad breath.

BULLY. I forgot to brush my teeth.

HESTER. Go head.

(Bully squats off in the "bathroom" and rubs her teeth with her finger.)

AMIGA GRINGA. Babys daddy, that Reverend, he ever give you money?

HESTER. No.

AMIGA GRINGA. He's a gold mine. I seen the collection plate going around. Its a full plate.

HESTER. I aint seen him since before Baby was born.

AMIGA GRINGA. Thats two years.

HESTER. He didnt want nothing to do with me. His heart went hard.

AMIGA GRINGA. My second kids daddy had a hard heart at first. But time mushed him up. Remember when he comed around crying about his lineage and asking whered the baby go?

And I'd already gived it up.

HESTER. Reverend D., his heart is real hard. Like a rock.

AMIGA GRINGA. Worth a try all the same.

HESTER. Yeah.

(Rest.)

Who told you Chilli was looking for me?

AMIGA GRINGA. Word on the street, thats all.

(Trouble, dressed in superhero pajamas, comes in. He holds a box of matches. He lights one.)

HESTER. What the hell you doing?

TROUBLE. Sleepwalking.

HESTER. You sleepwalk yrself back over here and gimmie them matches or Ima kill you.

(He gives her the matches. Bully has finished with her teeth.)

BULLY. You wanna smell?

HESTER. Thats ok.

BULLY. Dont you wanna smell?

(Hester leans in and Bully opens her mouth.)

I only did one side cause I only ate with one side today.

HESTER. Go on to bed.

(Bully passes Trouble and hits him hard.)

TROUBLE. Aaaaah!

BULLY. Yr a bad person!

(She hits him again.)

TROUBLE. Aaaaaaaaah!

HESTER. Who made you policewoman?

TROUBLE. Ima blow you sky high one day you bully bitch!

(Bully goes to hit him again.)

HESTER. Trouble I thought you said you was sleep. Go inside and lie down and shut up or you wont see tomorrow.

(He goes back to sleepwalking and goes inside.)

Bully. Go over there. Close yr eyes and yr mouth and not a word, hear?

(Bully goes a distance off curling up to sleep without a word.)

I used to wash Troubles mouth out with soap when he used bad words. Found out he likes the taste of soap. Sometimes you cant win. No matter what you do.

(Rest.)

19

Im gonna talk to Welfare and get an upgrade. The worldll take care of the women and children.

AMIGA GRINGA. Theyre gonna give you the test. See what skills you got. Make you write stuff.

HESTER. Like what?

AMIGA GRINGA. Like yr name.

HESTER. I can write my damn name. Im not such a fool that I cant write my own goddamn name. I can write my goddamn name.

(Inside, Baby starts crying.)

HUSH!

(Baby hushes.)

AMIGA GRINGA. You should pay yrself a visit to Babys daddy. Dont take along the kid in the flesh thatll be too much. For a buck I'll get someone to take a snapshot.

(Jabber comes in. He wears mismatched pajamas. He doesnt come too close but keeps his distance.)

JABBER. I was in a row boat and the sea was flat like a blue plate and you was rowing me and it was fun.

HESTER. Go back to bed.

JABBER. It was a good day but then Bad News and the sea started rolling and the boat tipped and I fell out and —

HESTER. You wet the bed.

JABBER. I fell out the boat.

HESTER. You wet the bed.

JABBER. I wet the bed.

HESTER. 13 years old still peeing in the bed.

JABBER. It was uh accident.

HESTER. Whats wrong with you?

JABBER. Accidents happen.

HESTER. Yeah you should know cause yr uh damn accident. Shit. Take that off.

(Jabber strips.)

AMIGA GRINGA. He aint bad looking, Hester. A little slow, but some women like that.

HESTER. Wear my coat. Gimmie a kiss.

(He puts on her coat and kisses her on the cheek.)

JABBER. Mommie?

HESTER. Bed.

JABBER. All our daddys died, right? All our daddys died in the war, right?

HESTER. Yeah, Jabber.

JABBER. They went to war and they died and you cried. They went to war and died but whered they go when they died?

HESTER. They into other things now.

JABBER. Like what?

HESTER. —. Worms. They all turned into worms, honey. They crawling around in the dirt happy as larks, eating the world up, never hungry. Go to bed.

(Jabber goes in.)

(Rest.)

AMIGA GRINGA. Worms?

HESTER. Whatever.

AMIGA GRINGA. He's yr favorite. You like him the best.

HESTER. He's my first.

AMIGA GRINGA. He's yr favorite.

HESTER. I dont got no *favorite.*

(Rest.)

5 bucks. 3 for their treats. And one for that photo. Reverend D. aint the man I knew. He's got money now. A salvation business and all. Maybe his stone-heart is mush, though. Maybe.

AMIGA GRINGA. Cant hurt to try.

SCENE 2
STREET PRACTICE

Hester walks alone down the street. She has a framed picture of Baby.

HESTER. Picture, it comed out pretty good. Got him sitting on a chair, and dont he look like he got everything one could want in life? He's two yrs old. Andll be growd up with a life of his own before I blink.

(Rest.)
Picture comed out good. Thought Amiga was cheating me but it comed out good.
(She meets the Doctor, coming the other way. As before he carries all of his office paraphernalia on his back. He wears a sandwich board with the words written on it hidden.)
DOCTOR. Hester. Dont move a muscle, I'll be set up in a jiffy.
HESTER. I dont got more than a minute.
DOCTOR. Hows yr gut?
HESTER. Not great.
DOCTOR. Say "Aaaah!"
HESTER. Aaaah!
(As she stands there with her mouth open, he sets up his roadside office: a thin curtain, his doctors shingle, his instruments, his black bag.)
DOCTOR. Good good good good good. Lets take yr temperature. Do you know what it takes to keep my road-side practice running? Do you know how much The Higher Ups would like to shut me down? Every blemish on your record is a blemish on mine. Take yr guts for instance. Yr pain could be nothing or it could be the end of the road — a cyst or a tumor, a lump or a virus or an infected sore. Or cancer, Hester. Undetected. There youd be, lying in yr coffin with all yr little ones gathered around motherlessly weeping and The Higher Ups pointing their fingers at me, saying I should of saved the day, but instead stood idly by. You and yr children live as you please and Im the one The Higher Ups hold responsible. Would you like a pill?
HESTER. No thanks. *(She doubles over in pain.)* My gut hurts.
(The Doctor takes a pill.)
DOCTOR. In a minute. We'll get to that in a minute. How are yr children?
HESTER. Theyre all right.
DOCTOR. All 5?
HESTER. All 5.
DOCTOR. Havent had any more have you?
HESTER. No.
DOCTOR. But you could. But you might.
HESTER. — Maybe.

DOCTOR. Word from The Higher Ups is that one more kid outa the likes of you and theyre on the likes of me like white on rice. I'd like to propose something —. Yr running a temperature. Bit of a fever. Whats this?

HESTER. Its a club. For protection.

DOCTOR. Good thinking.

(He examines her quickly and thoroughly.)

The Higher Ups are breathing down my back, Hester. They want answers! They want results! Solutions! Solutions! Solutions! Thats what they want.

(He goes to take another pill, but doesnt.)

I only take one a day. I only allow myself one a day.

(Rest.)

(He goes back to examining her.)

Breathe in deep. Lungs are clear. Yr heart sounds good. Strong as an ox.

HESTER. This falls been cold. The wind under the bridge is colder than the wind on the streets.

DOCTOR. Exercise. Thats what I suggest. When the temperature drops, I run in place. Hold yr hands out. Shaky. Experiencing any stress and tension?

HESTER. Not really.

DOCTOR. Howre yr meals?

HESTER. The kids come first.

DOCTOR. Course they do. Howre yr bowels. Regular?

HESTER. I dunno.

DOCTOR. Once a day?

HESTER. Sometimes. My gut —

DOCTOR. In a minute. Gimmie the Spread & Squat right quick. Lets have a look under the hood.

(Standing, Hester spreads her legs and squats. Like an otter, he slides between her legs on a dolly and looks up into her privates with a flashlight.)

Last sexual encounter?

HESTER. Thats been a while, now.

DOCTOR. Yve healed up well from yr last birth.

HESTER. Its been 2 years. His names Baby.

DOCTOR. Any pain, swelling, off-color discharge, strange smells?

HESTER. No.

DOCTOR. L.M.P.?

HESTER. About a week ago.

(Rest.)

How *you* been feeling, Doc?

DOCTOR. Sometimes Im up, sometimes Im down.

HESTER. You said you was lonesome once. I came for a checkup and you said you was lonesome. You lonesome today, Doc?

DOCTOR. No.

HESTER. Oh.

(Far away, Chilli walks by with his picnic basket on his arm. He pauses, checks his pocket watch, then continues on.)

DOCTOR. Yr intelligent. Attractive enough. You could of made something of yrself.

HESTER. Im doing all right.

DOCTOR. The Higher Ups say yr in a skid. I agree.

HESTER. Oh, I coulda been the Queen of Sheba, it just werent in the cards, Doc.

DOCTOR. Yr kids are 5 strikes against you.

HESTER. I dont need no lecture. Gimmie something for my gut so I can go.

DOCTOR. The Higher Ups, they say Im not making an impact. But what do you care.

HESTER. My gut —

DOCTOR. Stand right here.

(He draws a line in the dirt, positions her behind it and walks a few steps away. He reveals the writing on his sandwich board. It is an eye exam chart. The letters on the first line spell "SPAY.")

Read.

HESTER. —. A.

DOCTOR. Good.

(He takes a step closer decreasing the distance between them.)

Read.

HESTER. —. —. —.

(Rest.)

I need glasses for that.

DOCTOR. Uh huhn. *(He steps closer.)* How about now?

HESTER. I need glasses I guess.

DOCTOR. I guess you do.
(He steps even closer.)
HESTER. ((somethin-somethin-A-somethin.))
(Rest.)
I need glasses.
DOCTOR. You cant read this?
HESTER. I gotta go.
(She turns to go and he grabs her hand, holding her fast.)
DOCTOR. When I say removal of your "womanly parts" do you
know what parts Im talking about?
HESTER. Yr gonna take my womans parts?
DOCTOR. My hands are tied. The Higher Ups are calling the
shots now.
(Rest.)
You have 5 healthy children, itll be for the best, considering.
HESTER. My womans parts.
DOCTOR. Ive fowarded my recommendation to yr caseworker.
Its out of my hands. Im sorry.
HESTER. I gotta go.
(But she doesnt move. She stands there numbly.)
DOCTOR. Yr gut. Lets have a listen. *(He puts his ear to her stom-
ach and listens.)* Growling hungry stomach. Heres a dollar. Go get
yrself a sandwich.
(She takes the money and goes.)

DOCTOR.
DOCTOR.
DOCTOR.

First Confession: The Doctor
"Times Are Tough: What Can We Do?"

DOCTOR.
Times are tough:
What can we do?
When I see a woman begging on the streets I guess I could
Bring her in my house
sit her at my table
make her a member of my family, sure.
But there are hundreds and thousands of them
and my house cant hold them all.
Maybe we should all take in just one.
Except they wouldnt really fit.
They wouldnt really fit in with us.
Theres such a gulf between us. What can we do?
I am a man of the people from way back my streetside practice is
a testement to that
so dont get me wrong
do not for a moment think that I am one of those people haters
      who does not understand who does not experience — compassion.
(Rest.)
Shes been one of my neediest cases for several years now.
What can I do?
Each time she comes to me
looking more and more forlorn
and more and more in need
of affection.
At first I wouldnt touch her without gloves on, but then
(Rest.)
We did it once
in that alley there
she was
phenomenal.
(Rest.)
I was

lonesome and
She gave herself to me in a way that I had never experienced
even with women Ive paid
she was, like she was giving me something that was not hers to give
    me but something that was mine
that I'd lent her
and she was returning it to me.
Sucked me off for what seemed like hours
but I was very insistent. And held back
and she understood that I wanted her in the traditional way.
And she was very giving very motherly very obliging very
    understanding
very phenomenal.
Let me cumm inside her. Like I needed to.
What could I do?
I couldnt help it.

SCENE 3
THE REVEREND ON HIS SOAPBOX

*Late at night. The Reverend D. On his soapbox preaching to
no one in particular. There is a display of taped versions of
his sermons for sale.*

REVEREND D. You all know me. You all know this face. These
arms. These legs. This body of mine is known to you. To all of
you. There isnt a person on the street tonight that hasnt passed me
by at some point. Maybe when I was low, many years ago, with a
bottle in my hand and the cold hard unforgiving pavement for my
dwelling place. Perhaps you know me from that. Or perhaps you
know me from my more recent incarnation. The man on the
soapbox, telling you of a better life thats available to you, not after
the demise of your physical being, not in some heaven where we
all gonna be robed in satin sheets and wearing gossamer wings, but

right here on earth, my friends. Right here right now. Let the man on the soapbox tell you how to pick yourself up. Let the man on the soapbox tell you how all yr dreams can come true. Let the man on the soapbox tell you that you dont have to be down and dirty, you dont have to be ripped off and renounced, you dont have to be black and blue, your neck dont have to be red, your clothes dont have to be torn, your head dont have to be hanging, you dont have to *hate* yourself, you dont have to hate yr neighbor. You can pull yrself up.

(Hester comes in with a framed picture of Baby. She stands a ways off. Reverend D. keeps on talking.)

And I am an example of that. I am a man who has crawled out of the quicksand of despair. I am a man who has pulled himself out of that never ending gutter — and you notice friends that every city and every towns got a gutter. Aint no place in the world that dont have some little trench for its waste. And the gutter, is endless, and deep and wide and if you think you gonna crawl out of the gutter by crawling along the gutter you gonna be in the gutter for the rest of your life. You gotta step out of it, friends and I am here to tell you that you can.

(Rest.)

(He sees Hester but doesnt recognize her.)

What can I do for you tonight, my sister.

HESTER. I been good.

REVEREND D. But yr life is weighing heavy on you tonight.

HESTER. I havent bothered you.

REVEREND D. Reverend D. likes to be bothered. Reverend D. enjoys having the tired, the deprived and the depraved come knocking on his door. Come gathering around his soapbox. Come closer. Come on.

(Hester holds the picture of Baby in front of her face, hiding her face from view.)

HESTER. This child here dont know his daddy.

REVEREND D. The ultimate disaster of modern times. Sweet child. Yours?

HESTER. Yes.

REVEREND D. Do you know the father?

HESTER. Yes.

REVEREND D. You must go to him and say "Mister, here is your child!"
HESTER. Mister here is your child!
REVEREND D. "You are wrong to deny what God has made!"
HESTER. You are wrong to deny what God has made!
REVEREND D. "He has nothing but love for you and reaches out his hands every day crying wheres daddy?"
HESTER. Wheres daddy?
REVEREND D. "Wont you answer those cries?"
HESTER. Wont you answer those cries?
REVEREND D. If he dont respond to that then he's a good-for-nothing deadbeat, and you report him to the authorities. Theyll garnish his wages so at least you all wont starve. I have a motivational cassette which speaks to that very subject. I'll give it to you free of charge.
HESTER. I got all yr tapes. I send my eldest up here to get them.
REVEREND D. Wonderful. Thats wonderful. You should go to yr childs father and demand to be recognized.
HESTER. Its been years since I seen him. He didnt want me bothering him so I been good.
REVEREND D. Go to him. Plead with him. Show him this sweet face and yours. He cannot deny you.
(Hester lowers the picture, revealing her face.)

HESTER.
REVEREND D.
HESTER.
REVEREND D.

(Rest.)
HESTER. You know me?
REVEREND D. No. God.
HESTER. I aint bothered you for 2 years.
REVEREND D. You should go. Home. Let me call you a taxi. *Taxi!* You shouldnt be out this time of night. Young mother like you. In a neighborhood like this. We'll get you home in a jiff. Where ya live? East? West? North I bet, am I right? *TAXI!* God.
HESTER. He's talking now. Not much but some. He's a good boy.

29

REVEREND D. I am going to send one of my people over to your home tomorrow. Theyre marvelous, the people who work with me. Theyll put you in touch with all sorts of agencies that can help you. Get some food in that stomach of yours. Get you some sleep.

HESTER. Doctor says I got a fever. We aint doing so good. We been slipping. I been good. I dont complain. They breaking my back is all. 5 kids. My treasures, breaking my back.

REVEREND D. We'll take up a collection for you.

HESTER. You know me.

REVEREND D. You are under the impression that —. Your mind, having nothing better to fix itself on has fixed on me. Me, someone youve never even met.

HESTER. There aint no one here but you and me. Say it. You know me. You know my name. You know my —. You know me and I know you.

HESTER.
REVEREND D.

(Rest.)

REVEREND D. Here is a card. My lawyer. He'll call you.

HESTER. We dont got no phone.

REVEREND D. He'll visit. Write yr address on —. Tell me yr address. I'll write it down. I'll give it to him in the morning and he'll visit you.

(Rest.)

Do the authorities know the name of the father?

HESTER. I dont tell them nothing.

REVEREND D. They would garnish his wages if you did. That would provide you with a small income. If you agree not to ever notify the authorities, we could, through my instutition, arrange for you to get a much larger amount of money.

HESTER. How much more?

REVEREND D. Twice as much.

HESTER. 3 times.

REVEREND D. Fine.

HESTER. Theres so many things we need. Food. New shoes. A regular dinner with meat and salad and bread.

REVEREND D. I should give you some money right now. As a promise to you that I'll keep my word. But Im short of cash.
HESTER. Oh.
REVEREND D. Come back in two days. Late. I'll have some then.
HESTER. You dont got no food or nothing do ya?
REVEREND D. Come back in two days. Not early. Late. And not a word to no one. Okay?
HESTER. —. K.

REVEREND D.
HESTER.
REVEREND D.
HESTER.

(Rest.)
REVEREND D. You better go.
(Hester goes.)

SCENE 4
WITH THE WELFARE

Outside, Jabber, Trouble and Beauty sit in the dirt playing with toy cars.

TROUBLE. Green light. Red light. Greet light. Red light.
JABBER. Look, a worm.
(They all study the worm as it writhes in the dirt. Welfare enters.)
WELFARE. Wheres your mommie?
BEAUTY. Inside.
JABBER. Mommie! Welfares here.
WELFARE. Thank you.
(Hester enters.)
HESTER. You all go inside.
(The kids go inside.)

31

WELFARE. Hands clean?
HESTER. Yes, Maam.
WELFARE. Wash them again.
(Hester washes her hands again. Dries them.)
The welfare of the world.
HESTER. Maam?
WELFARE. Come on over, come on.
(Hester stands behind Welfare, giving her a shoulder rub.)
The welfare of the world weighs on these shoulders, Hester.
(Rest.)
We at Welfare are at the end of our rope with you, Hester. We put
you in a job and you quit. We put you in a shelter and you walk.
We put you in school and you drop out. Yr children are also tru-
ant. Word is they steal. Stealing is a gateway crime, Hester. Perhaps
your young daughter is pregnant. Who knows. We build bridges
you burn them. We sew safety nets, rub harder, good strong safety
nets and you slip through the weave.
HESTER. We was getting by all right, then I dunno, I been tired
lately. Like something in me broke.
WELFARE. You and yr children live, who knows where.
HESTER. Here Maam, under the Main Bridge.
WELFARE. This is not the country, Hester. You cannot simply
— live off the land. If yr hungry you go to the shelter and get a
hot meal.
HESTER. The shelter hassles me. Always prying in my business.
Stealing my shit. Touching my kids. We was making ends meet all
right then — ends got further apart.
WELFARE. "Ends got further apart." God!
(Rest.)
I care because it is my job to care. I am paid to stretch out these
hands, Hester. Stretch out these hands. To you.
HESTER. I gived you the names of 4 daddys: Jabbers and Bullys
and Troubles and Beautys. You was gonna find them. Garnish
they wages.
WELFARE. No luck as yet but we're looking. Sometimes these
searches take years.
HESTER. Its been years.
WELFARE. Lifetimes then. Sometimes they take that long. These

men of yours, theyre deadbeats. They dont want to be found. Theyre probably all in Mexico wearing false mustaches. Ha ha ha.
(Rest.)
What about the newest child?
HESTER. Baby.
WELFARE. What about "Babys" father?
HESTER. —. I dunno.
WELFARE. Dont know or dont remember?
HESTER. You think Im doing it with mens I dont know?
WELFARE. No need to raise your voice no need of that at all. You have to help me help you, Hester.
(Rest.)
Run yr fingers through my hair. Go on. Feel it. Silky isnt it?
HESTER. Yes Maam.
WELFARE. Comes from a balanced diet. Three meals a day. Strict adherence to the food pyramid. Money in my pocket, clothes on my back, teeth in my mouth, womanly parts where they should be, hair on my head, husband in my bed.
(Hester combs Welfares hair.)
Yr doctor recommends that you get a hysterectomy. Take out yr womans parts. A spay.
HESTER. Spay.
WELFARE. I hope things wont come to that. I will do what I can. But you have to help me out, Hester.
HESTER. ((Dont *make* me hurt you.).)
WELFARE. What?
HESTER. I didnt mean it. Just slipped out.
WELFARE. Remember yr manners. We worked good and hard on yr manners. Remember? Remember that afternoon over at my house? That afternoon with the teacups?
HESTER. *Manners*, Maam?
WELFARE. Yes. Manners.

HESTER.
WELFARE.

WELFARE. Babys daddy. Whats his name?
HESTER. You wont find him no how.

33

WELFARE. We could get lucky. He could be right around the corner and I could walk out and there he would be and then we at Welfare would wrestle him to the ground and turn him upside down and let you and yr Baby grab all the money that falls from Deadbeat Daddys pockets. I speak metaphorically. We would garnish his wages.

HESTER. How much would that put in my pocket?

WELFARE. Depends how much he earns. Maybe 100. Maybe. We take our finders fee. Whats his name?

HESTER. I dunno.

WELFARE. You dont have to say it out loud. Write it down.

(She gives Hester pencil and paper. Hester writes. Welfare looks at the paper.)

"A."

(Rest.)

Adam, Andrew, Archie, Arthur, Aloysius, "A" what?

HESTER. Looks good dont it?

WELFARE. You havent learned yr letters yet, have you?

HESTER. I want my leg up is all.

WELFARE. You wont get something for nothing.

HESTER. I been good.

WELFARE. 5 bastards is not good. 5 bastards is bad.

HESTER. Dont make me hurt you!

(Hester raises her club to strike Welfare.)

WELFARE. You hurt me and, kids or no kids, I'll have you locked up. We'll take yr kids away and yll never see them again.

HESTER. My lifes my own fault. I know that. But the world dont help, Maam.

WELFARE. The world is not here to help us, Hester. The world is simply here. We must help ourselves.

(Rest.)

I know just the job for you. It doesnt pay well, but the work is very rewarding. Hard honest work. Unless yr afraid of hard honest work.

HESTER. I aint afraid of hard work.

WELFARE. Its sewing. You can do it at home. No work no pay but thats yr decision.

(Rest.)

Heres the fabric. Make sure you dont get it dirty.

HESTER. Can I express myself?
WELFARE. Needles, thread and the pattern, in this bag. Take the cloth. Sew it. If you do a good job therell be more work. Have it sewn by tomorrow morning, yll get a bonus.
(Hester takes the cloth and notions.)
HESTER. I dont think the world likes women much.
WELFARE. Dont be silly.
HESTER. I was just thinking.
WELFARE. Im a woman too! And a black woman too just like you. Dont be silly.

HESTER.
WELFARE.

(Rest.)
(Hester puts her hand out, waiting.)
HESTER. Yr shoulders. Plus I did yr hair.
WELFARE. Is a buck all right?

HESTER.
WELFARE.

WELFARE. Unless yll change a 50.
HESTER. I could go get change —
WELFARE. Take the buck, K? And the cloth. And go.
(Welfare owes Hester more $, but after a beat, Hester just leaves.)

Second Confession: The Welfare
"I Walk The Line"

WELFARE.
I walk the line
between us and them
between our kind and their kind.
The balance of the system depends on a well-drawn boundary line
And all parties respecting that boundary.
I am
I am a married woman.
I dont — that is have never
never in the past or even in the recent present or even when I look
look out into the future of my life I do not see any interest
any *sexual* interest
in anyone
other than my husband.
(Rest.)
My dear husband.
The hours he keeps.
The money he brings home.
Our wonderful children.
The vacations we go on.
My dear husband he needed
a little spice.
And I agreed. We both needed spice.
We both hold very demanding jobs.
We put an ad in the paper: "Husband and Bi-Curious Wife,
    seeking — "
But the women we got:
Hookers. Neurotics. Gold diggers!
"Bring one of those gals home from work," hubby said. And
Hester,
she came to tea.
(Rest.)
She came over and we had tea.

From my mothers china.
And marzipan on matching china plates.
Hubby sat opposite in the recliner
hard as Gibralter. He told us what he wanted and we did it.
We were his little puppets.
She was surprised, but consented.
Her body is better than mine.
Not a single stretchmark on her
Im a looker too dont get me wrong just in a different way and
Hubby liked the contrast.
Just light petting at first.
Running our hands on each other
Then Hubby joined in
And while she and I kissed
Hubby did her and me alternately.
The thrill of it — .
(Rest.)
I was so afraid I'd catch something
But I was swept away and couldnt stop
She stuck her tongue down my throat
And Hubby doing his thing on top
my skin shivered
She let me slap her across the face
and I crossed the line.
(Rest.)
It was my first threesome
And it wont happen again.
And I should emphasize that
she is a low-class person.
What I mean by that is that we have absolutely nothing in common.
As her caseworker I realize that maintenance of the system depends
on a well-drawn boundary line
And all parties respecting that boundary.
And I am, after all,
I am a married woman.
(Welfare exits. Hester reenters to watch Welfare exit.)
HESTER. Bitch.
(Hester, alone on stage, examines the cloth Welfare gave her.)

Sure is pretty cloth. Sewing cant be that hard. Thread the needle stick it in and pull it through. Pretty cloth. Lets see what we making. Oooooh. Uh evening dress. Go to a party in. Drink champagne and shit. Uh huh, "Dont mind if I do," and shit and la de *dah* and come up in a limo and everybody wants a picture. So many lights Im blinded. Wear dark glasses. Strut my stuff. *(She has another painful stomach attack which knocks the wind out of her and doubles her over. Far away, Chilli walks by with his picnic basket on his arm. He pauses, checks his pocket watch, then continues on. Hester, recovering from her attack, sees him just before he disappears.)* Chilli!

INTERMISSION

SCENE 5
SMALL CHANGE AND SANDWICHES

*Late at night. The children inside, all sleeping. Lots of "A"s
written in Hesters practice place.*

Hester, working on her sewing, tries to thread the needle.

HESTER. Damn needle eyes too damn small. Howmy supposed
to get the thread through. Theres a catch to everything, Hester. No
easy money nowheres. Wet the thread good. Damn.
*(She squeezes her eyes shut and opens them, trying to focus. Having dif-
ficulty threading the needle, she takes out an object wrapped in brown
paper. Looks cautiously around. Begins to unwrap it. A sandwich.)*
Put something in my stomach maybe my eyesll work.
*(Amiga Gringa comes in. Hester stashes the package, picks up her
sewing.)*
AMIGA GRINGA. Mother Hubbard sewing by street lamp. Very
moving.
HESTER. I got me uh job. This here is work.
AMIGA GRINGA. From Welfare?
HESTER. Shes getting me back in the workforce. I do good on
this she'll give me more.
AMIGA GRINGA. Whats the pay?
HESTER. Its by the piece.
AMIGA GRINGA. How much?
HESTER. 10 bucks maybe.
AMIGA GRINGA. Maybe?
HESTER. I get a bonus for working fast.
AMIGA GRINGA. Very nice fabric. Very pretty. Very expensive.
And oooh, look at what yr making.
HESTER. You good with needles? Thread this. My eyes aint good.
(Amiga tries halfheartedly to thread the needle. Quits.)
AMIGA GRINGA. Sorry.

(Hester continues trying to thread the needle.)
Good yr working. Getting some money in yr pocket. Making a good example for the kids. Pulling yrself up by yr bootstraps. Getting with the program. Taking responsibility for yr life. I envy you.
HESTER. Me?
AMIGA GRINGA. Yr working, Im — looking for work.
HESTER. I bet I could get you some sewing.
AMIGA GRINGA. Oh no. Thats not for me. If I work, Hester, I would want to be paid a living wage. You have agreed to work for less than a living wage. May as well be a slave. Or an animal.
HESTER. Its a start. She said if I do well —
AMIGA GRINGA. If you do well shes gonna let you be her slave *for life*. Wouldnt catch me doing that. Chump work. No no no. But its a good thing you are. Example to the kids.
HESTER. I aint no chump.
AMIGA GRINGA. Course you arent. Yr just doing chump work is all.
HESTER. Its a leg up. Cant start from the top.
AMIGA GRINGA. Why not? Plenty of people start from the top. Why not you? Sure is pretty fabric.
HESTER. All I gotta do is sew along the lines.
AMIGA GRINGA. Bet the fabric cost a lot. I wonder how much we could get for it — on the open market.
HESTER. Aint mine to sell. Its gonna make a nice dress. Im gonna sew it up and try it on before I give it to her. Just for fun.
(But Hester still hasnt been able to thread the needle.)
AMIGA GRINGA. Bet we could get 100 bucks. For the fabric. A lot more than youd get for sewing it. And you wouldnt have to lift a finger. Id sell it tonight. Have the money for you in the morning.
HESTER. No thanks.
AMIGA GRINGA. Suit yrself.
(Hester contiues trying to thread that damn needle.)
Chump work.
HESTER. They make the eyes too small, thats the problem.
(Rest.)
I seen Chilli right after I was with the Welfare. You said he was looking for me and there he was! Jabbers daddy walking right by

with a big gold pocket watch. But did I tell? Did I run after Welfare and say "Theres Jabbers daddy?" I did not. Can you imagine?

AMIGA GRINGA. I told ya he was looking for ya. He's gonna find you too.

HESTER. Jabbers daddy, after all these years!

AMIGA GRINGA. Maybe yr lucks turning.

HESTER. You think?

AMIGA GRINGA. Maybe.

AMIGA GRINGA.
HESTER.

(Rest.)

AMIGA GRINGA. I missed my period.

HESTER. Dont look at *me*.

(Rest.)

Whatcha gonna do.

AMIGA GRINGA. Have it, I guess.

HESTER. You may not be knocked up.

AMIGA GRINGA. Theres something in here all right. I can feel it growing inside. Just my luck.

HESTER. You shoulda been careful.

AMIGA GRINGA. — Whatever.

HESTER. So get rid of it if you dont want it.

AMIGA GRINGA. Or birth it then sell it.

HESTER. You as crazy as they come.

AMIGA GRINGA.
HESTER.
AMIGA GRINGA.

(Amiga leans toward Hester to kiss her. Hester pulls back a bit.)

AMIGA GRINGA. Whassamatter?

HESTER. I dont got no love for nobody cept the kids.

(Amiga pulls back, takes up the fabric.)

AMIGA GRINGA. I'll get you a lot of money for this.

HESTER. No.

AMIGA GRINGA. Whassis?

41

(Shes discovered the brown paper package.)
HESTER. Nothing.
AMIGA GRINGA. Smells like something. Smells like food. Smells like egg salad.
HESTER. I was saving it.
AMIGA GRINGA. Lets celebrate! Come on itll be fun. Kids!
HESTER. They *sleep*. Let em sleep.
AMIGA GRINGA. Lets toast my new kid. Just you and me. A new life has begun. Am I showing? Not yet, right? Will be soon enough. Little Bastards in there living high on the hog, taking up space. Little Bastard, we toast you with: egg salad.
(Amiga takes a big bite out of the sandwich. Hester grabs at it but Amiga keeps it from her reach. Bully comes outside.)
BULLY. Mommie?
HESTER. Yes, Bully.
BULLY. My hands.
HESTER. Lemmie unlock em.
(Bully comes over. Hester opens her hands.)
BULLY. Egg salad?
AMIGA GRINGA. Yeah. Its yr mommies sandwich.
(Amiga gives the sandwich to Hester who almost takes a bite but sees Bully looking on hungrily. She gives the sandwich to Bully. Bully eats. Hester gives Amiga the fabric.)
HESTER. Cheat me and I'll kill you.
AMIGA GRINGA. Have a little faith, Hester. Amiga will sell this fabric for you. You will not be a chump. In the morning when the sun comes up yll be 100 bucks richer. Sleep tight.
(Amiga takes the fabric and leaves. Bully sitting with her mother, licking her fingers.)

Third Confession: Amiga Gringa
"In My Head I Got It Going On"

AMIGA GRINGA.
In my head I got it going on.
The triple X rated movie:
Hester and Amiga get down and get dirty.
Chocolate and Vanilla get into the ugly.
We coulda done a sex show behind a curtain
Then make a movie and sell it
for 3 bucks a peek.
I had me some delicious schemes
to get her out of that hole she calls home.
Im doing well for myself
working my money maker
Do you have any idea how much cash I'll get for the fruit of my
    white womb?!
Grow it.
Birth it.
Sell it.
And why shouldnt I?
(Rest.)
Funny how a woman like Hester
driving her life all over the road
most often chooses to walk the straight and narrow.
Girl on girl action is a very lucrative business.
And someones gotta do something for her.
Im just trying to help her out.
And myself too, ok. They dont call it Capitalizm for nothing.
(Rest.)
She liked the idea of the sex
at least she acted like it.
Her looking at me with those eyes of hers
You looking like you want it, Hester
Shoot, Miga, she says thats just the way I look she says.
It took a little cajoling to get her to do it with me

For an invited audience.
For a dime a look.
Over at my place.
Every cent was profit and no overhead to speak of.
The guys in the neighborhood got their pleasure
and we was our own boss so we didnt have to pay no joker off the top.
We slipped right into a very profitable situation
like sliding into warm water.
Her breasts her bottom
She let me touch her however I wanted
I let her ride my knees
She made sounds like an animal.
She put her hand between my legs.
One day some of the guys took advantage.
Ah, what do you expect in a society based on Capitalizm.
I tell you the plight of the worker these days — .
Still one day Im gonna get her to make the movie
Cause her and me we had the moves down
very sensual, very provocative, very scientific, very lucrative.
In my head I got it going on.

SCENE 6
THE REVEREND ON THE ROCK

*Late at night. Down the road, Reverend D., cleaning his
cornerstone, a white block of granite with the date in Roman
numerals, and practicing his preaching.*

[REVEREND D. "It is easier for a camel to go through the eye
of a needle than for a rich man to enter the kingdom of God." And
you hear that and you say, let me get a tax shelter and hide some
of my riches so that when I stand up there in judgment, God wont
be none the wiser! And that is the problem with the way we see
God. For most of us, God is like the IRS. God garnishes yr wages

44

if you dont pay up. God withholds. The wages of sin, they lead to death, so you say, let me give to the poor. But not any poor, just those respectable charities. I want my poor looking good. I want my poor to know that it was me who bought the such and such. I want my poor on tv. I want famous poor, not miscellaneous poor. And I dont want local poor. Local poor dont look good. Gimmie foreign poor. Poverty exotica. Gimmie brown and yellow skins against a non-western landscape, some savanna, some rain forest some rice paddy. Gimmie big sad eyes with the berri-berri belly and the outstretched hands struggling to say "Thank-You" the only english they know, right into the camera. And put me up there with them, holding them, comforting them, telling them everythings gonna be alright, we gonna raise you up, we gonna get you on the bandwagon of our ways, put a smile in yr heart and a hamburger in yr belly, baby.

(Rest.)

And that is how we like our poor. At arms length. Like a distant relation with no complication. But folks, we gotta —]

(Hester comes in and watches him. After a while, he notices her and stops talking.)

HESTER. Nice rock.

REVEREND D. Thank you.

HESTER. Theres writing on it.

REVEREND D. Dont come close. Its the date its just the date. The date. Well, the year.

HESTER. Like a calendar.

REVEREND D. Its a cornerstone. The first stone of my new church. My backers are building me a church and this is the first stone.

HESTER. Oh.

(Rest.)

You told me to come back. Im back.

REVEREND D. Theyll start building my church tomorrow. My church will be a beautiful place. Its not much of a neighborhood now but when my church gets built, oh therell be a turnaround. Lots of opportunity for everyone. I feel like one of the pilgrims. You know, they step out of their boats and on to that Plymouth rock. I step off my soapbox and on to my cornerstone.

HESTER. You said come back to get my money. Im back.

REVEREND D. Do you know what a "Backer" is?

HESTER. Uh-uhn.

REVEREND D. Its a person who backs you. A person who believes in you. A person who looks you over and figures you just might make something of yrself. And they get behind you. With kind words, connections to high places, money. But they want to make sure they havent been suckered, so they watch you real close, to make sure yr as good as they think you are. To make sure you wont screw up and shame them and waste their money.

(Rest.)

My Backers are building me a church. It will be beautiful. And to make sure theyre not wasting their money on a man who was only recently a neerdowell, they watch me.

HESTER. They watching now?

REVEREND D. Not now. Now theyre in their nice beds. Between the cool sheets. Fast asleep. I dont sleep. I have this feeling that if I sleep I will miss someone. Someone in desperate need of what I have to say.

HESTER. Someone like me.

REVEREND D. I dont have your money yet but I will. I'll take up a collection for you on Sunday. I'll tell them yr story, that yr someone in need, and all the money will go to you. Every cent of it. We get good crowds on Sunday.

(Rest.)

Ive got work to do.

(He waits for her to go but she stays. He goes back to cleaning his cornerstone.)

HESTER. Today we had uh E-clipse. You seen it?

REVEREND D. You should go.

HESTER. A shadow passed over the sky. Everything was dark. For a minute.

REVEREND D. It was a cloud. Or an airplane. Happens all the time.

HESTER. No clouds out today. It was uh E-clipse.

REVEREND D. I am taking a collection for you on Sunday. Youll have to wait until then. Good night.

HESTER. Uh E-clipse.

REVEREND D. There was no eclipse today! No eclipse!
(Rest.)
Good night.
HESTER. I was crossing the street with the kids. We had a walk sign. White is walk and red is dont walk. I know white from red. Aint colorblind, right? And we was crossing. And a shadow fell over, everything started going dark and, shoot I had to look up. They say when theres uh *E*-clipse you shouldnt look up cause then you go blind and alls I need is to go blind, thank you. But I couldnt help myself. And so I stopped right there in the street and looked up. Never seen nothing like it.
(Rest.)
I dont know what I expected to see but.
(Rest.)
It was a big dark thing. Blocking the sun out. Like the hand of fate. The hand of fate with its 5 fingers coming down on me.
(Rest.)
(Rest.)
And then the trumpets started blaring.
(Rest.)
And then there was Jabber saying "Come on Mommie, Come on!" The trumpets was the taxi cabs. Wanting to run me over. Get out the road.

REVEREND D.
HESTER.
REVEREND D.
HESTER.

(Reverend D. sits on his rock, his back hiding his behavior which has become unseemly.)
REVEREND D. Comeer.
(Hester slowly goes to him.)
Suck me off.
HESTER. No.
REVEREND D. Itll only take a minute. Im halfway there. Please.
(She goes down on him. Briefly. He cumms. Mildly. Into his handkerchief. She stands there. Ashamed. Expectant.)

47

Go home. Put yr children to bed.
HESTER. Maybe we could get something regular going again —
REVEREND D. Go home. Go home.

HESTER.
REVEREND D.

(Rest.)
REVEREND D. Heres something. Its all I have.
(He offers her a crumpled bill which she takes.)
Next time you come by —. It would be better if you could come
around to the *back*. My churchll be going up and —. If you want
your money, it would be better if you come around to the back.
HESTER. Yeah.
(She goes. He sits there, watching her leave.)

Fourth Confession: Reverend D.
"Suffering Is An Enormous Turn-On"

REVEREND D.
Suffering is an enormous turn-on.
(Rest.)
She had four kids and she came to me asking me what to do.
She had a look in her eye that invites liaisons
Eyes that say red spandex.
She had four children four fatherless children four fatherless
mouths to feed
fatherless mouths fatherless mouths.
Add insult to injury was what I was thinking.
There was a certain animal magnetism between us.
And she threw herself at me
Like a baseball in the minors
fast but not deadly
I coulda stepped aside but.
God made her
and her fatherless mouths.
(Rest.)

I was lying in the never ending gutter of the street of the world.
You can crawl along it forever and never crawl out
praying for God to take my life
You can take it God
You can take my life back
you can have it
before I hurt myself somebody
before I do a damage that I cannot undo
before I do a crime that I can never pay for
In the never ending blistering heat
of the never ending gutter of the world
my skin hot against the pavement
but lying there I knew
that I had never hurt anybody in my life.
(Rest.)
(Rest.)
She was one of the multitude. She did not stand out.
(Rest.)
The intercourse was not memorable.
And when she told me of her *predicament*
I gave her enough money to take care of it.
(Rest.)
In all my days in the gutter I never hurt anyone.
I never held hate for anyone.
And now the hate I have for her
and her hunger
and the *hate* I have for her hunger.
God made me.
God pulled me up.
Now God, through her, wants to drag me down
and sit me at the table
at the head of the table of her fatherless house.

SCENE 7
MY SONG IN THE STREET

Hester with the kids. They are all playing freeze tag. After a bit, Hester is "it." She runs then stops, standing stock still, looking up into the sky. Bully gets tagged.

BULLY. 1 Mississippi, 2 Mississippi, 3 Mississippi, 4 Mississippi, 5 Mississippi.
(Jabber gets tagged.)
JABBER. 1 Mississippi, 2 Mississippi, 3 Mississippi, 4 Mississippi, 5 Mississippi. Yr it.
(Hester gets tagged.)

HESTER.
HESTER.

JABBER. Mommie?
HESTER. What.
BULLY. Whasswrong?
HESTER. You think I like you bothering me all day?

HESTER.
JABBER/BULLY/TROUBLE/BEAUTY.

(Rest.)
HESTER. All yall. Leave Mommie be. She cant play right now. Shes tired.
(Hester stands there looking up into the sky. The kids play apart.)
BULLY. Lemmie see it.
TROUBLE. What?
BULLY. Yr pee.

TROUBLE.

BULLY.

BULLY. Dont got no hair or nothing on it yet. I got hair on mines. Look.

TROUBLE.
BULLY.

TROUBLE. Jabber. Lets see yrs.

TROUBLE.
JABBER.
BULLY.

BULLY. Its got hair. Not as much as mines though.
BEAUTY. I had hairs but they fell out.
TROUBLE. Like a bald man or something?
BEAUTY. Yeah.

TROUBLE.
TROUBLE.

BULLY. Dont be touching yrself like that, Trouble, dont be nasty.

TROUBLE.
TROUBLE.

JABBER. You keep playing with it ssgonna fall off. Yr pee be laying in the street like a dead worm.
TROUBLE. Mommieeee!
HESTER. Dont talk to Mommie just now.
BULLY. Shes having a nervous breakdown.
HESTER. Shut the fuck up, please.
(Rest.)
(Rest.)
JABBER. When I grow up I aint never gonna use mines.
TROUBLE. Not me. I be *using* mines.
JABBER. Im gonna keep mines in my pants.

BULLY. How you ever gonna get married?

JABBER. Im gonna get married but Im gonna keep it in my pants.

BULLY. When you get married you gonna have to get on top uh yr wife.

JABBER. I'll get on top of her all right but I'll keep it in my pants.

TROUBLE. Jabber, you uh tragedy.

BULLY. When I get married my husbands gonna get on top of me and —

HESTER. No ones getting on top of you, Bully.

BULLY. He'll put the ring on my finger and I'll have me uh white dress and he'll get on top of me —

HESTER. No ones getting on top of you, Bully, no ones getting on top of you, so shut yr mouth about it.

TROUBLE. How she gonna have babies if no one gets on top of her?

HESTER. Dont *make* me hurt you!

(She raises her hand to Trouble who runs off. Bully starts crying.)

Shut the fuck up or I'll give you something to cry about!

(The kids huddle together in a knot.)

HESTER.
JABBER/BULLY/BEAUTY.
HESTER.
JABBER/BULLY/BEAUTY.
HESTER.

(Rest.)

HESTER. Bedtime.

BEAUTY. Its too early for bed —

HESTER. *BEDTIME!*

(They hurry off. Hester goes back to contemplating the sky.)

HESTER.
HESTER.
HESTER.

HESTER. Big dark thing. Gods hand. Coming down on me. Blocking the light out. Five-fingered hand of fate. Coming down on me.

(The Doctor comes on wearing his "SPAY" sandwich board. He watches her looking up. After a bit he looks up too.)
DOCTOR. We've scheduled you in for the day after tomorrow. First thing in the morning. You can send yr kids off to school then come on in. We'll have childcare for the baby. We'll give you good meals during yr recovery. Yll go to sleep. Yll go to sleep and when you wake up, whisk! Yll be all clean. No worries no troubles no trials no tribulations no more mistakes. Clean as a whistle. You wont feel a thing. Day after tomorrow. First thing in the morning. Free of charge. Itll be our pleasure. And yours. All for the best. In the long run, Hester. Congratulations.
(He walks off. Hester is still looking up. Chilli walks in with his picnic basket on his arm. He pauses to check his pocket watch. Hester lowers her head. The sight of him knocks the wind out of her.)
HESTER. Oh.
CHILLI. Ive been looking for you.
HESTER. Oh.
CHILLI. Ssbeen a long time.
HESTER. I — I —.
CHILLI. No need to speak.
HESTER. I —
CHILLI. Yr glad to see me.
HESTER. Yeah.
CHILLI. I been looking for you. Like I said. Lifes been good to me. Hows life been to you?
HESTER. Ok. —. Hard.

CHILLI.
HESTER.

HESTER. I was with the Welfare and I seed you. I called out yr name.
CHILLI. I didnt hear you. Darn.
HESTER. Yeah.
(Rest.)
I woulda run after you but —
CHILLI. But you were weak in the knees. And you couldnt move a muscle.

53

HESTER. Running after you woulda gived you away. And Welfares been after me to know the names of my mens.
CHILLI. Mens? More than one?
HESTER. I seed you and I called out yr name but I didnt run after you.
(Rest.)
You look good. I mean you always looked good but now you look better.
(Rest.)
I didnt run after you. I didnt give you away.
CHILLI. Thats my girl.
(Rest.)
Welfare has my name on file, though, doesnt she?
HESTER. From years ago. I —
CHILLI. Not to worry couldnt be helped. I changed my name. Theyll never find me. Theres no trace of the old me left anywhere.
HESTER. Cept Jabber.
CHILLI. Who?
HESTER. Yr son.

HESTER.
CHILLI.

CHILLI. Guess what time it is?
HESTER. He takes after you.
CHILLI. Go on guess. Betcha cant guess. Go on.
HESTER. Noon?
CHILLI. Lets see. I love doing this. I love guessing the time and then pulling out my watch and seeing how close I am or how far off. I love it. I spend all day doing it. Doctor says its a tick. A sure sign of some disorder. But I cant help it. And it doesnt hurt anyone. You guessed?
HESTER. Noon.
CHILLI. Lets see. Ah! 3.
HESTER. Oh.
CHILLI. Sorry.
(Rest.)
Whats up there?

HESTER. Nothing.

CHILLI. I want you to look at me. I want you to take me in. Ive been searching for you for weeks now and now Ive found you. I wasnt much when you knew me. When we knew each other I was — I was a shit.

(Rest.)

I was a shit, wasnt I?

HESTER.
CHILLI.

CHILLI. I was a shit, agree with me.

HESTER. We was young.

CHILLI. We was young. We had a romance. We had a love affair. We was young. We was in love. I was infatuated with narcotics. I got you knocked up then I split.

HESTER. Jabber, he's yr spitting image. Only he's a little slow, but —

CHILLI. Who?

HESTER. Jabber. Yr son.

CHILLI. Dont bring him into it just yet. I need time. Time to get to know you again. We need time alone together. Guess.

HESTER. 3:02.

CHILLI. Ah! 3:05. But better, yr getting better. Things move so fast these days. Ive seen the world Ive made some money Ive made a new name for myself and I have a loveless life. I dont have love in my life. Do you know what thats like? To be alone? Without love?

HESTER. I got my childr — I got Jabber. He's my treasure.

HESTER.
CHILLI.

(Rest.)

CHILLI. Im looking for a wife.

HESTER. Oh.

CHILLI. I want you to try this on.

(He takes a wedding dress out of his basket. He puts it on her, right over her old clothes. Hester rearranges the club, still held in her belt,

to get the dress on more securely.)

HESTER. I seed you and I called out your name, but you didnt hear me, and I wanted to run after you but I was like, Hester, if Welfare finds out Chillis in town they gonna give him hell so I didnt run. I didnt move a muscle. I was mad at you. Years ago. Then I seed you and I was afraid I'd never see you again and now here you are.

CHILLI. What do you think?

HESTER. Its so clean.

CHILLI. It suits you.

(Getting her shoes.)

HESTER. I got some special shoes. Theyd go good with this. Jabber, come meet yr daddy!

CHILLI. Not yet, kid!

(Rest.)

Lets not bring him into this just yet, K?

(He fiddles with his watch.)

14 years ago. Back in the old neighborhood. You and me and the moon and the stars. What was our song?

HESTER.
CHILLI.

HESTER. Huh?

CHILLI. What was our song?

(Rest.)

Da dee dah, dah dah dee dee?

HESTER. Its been a long time.

CHILLI. Listen.

(He plays their song, "The Looking Song," on a tinny tape recorder. He sings along as she stands there. After a bit he dances and gets her to dance with him. They sing as they dance and do a few moves from the old days.)

The Looking Song

Im looking for someone
to lose my looks with
looking for someone
to lose my shape with

looking for someone
to-get-my-hip-replaced with
looking for someone
Could it be you?

Im looking for someone
to lose my teeth with
looking for someone
to go stone deef with
looking for someone
to-lie-6-feet-underneath with
looking for someone
Could it be you?

They say "seek and you shall find"
So I will look until Im blind
Through this big old universe
For rich or poor better or worse
Singing:
Yuck up my tragedy
Oh darling, marry me
Walk down the aisle, walk on
Down Down Down

Yeah Im looking for someone
to lose my looks with
looking for someone
to lose my teeth with
looking for someone
I'll-lie-6-feet-underneath-with
looking for someone
Could it be you?

(Theyre breathless from dancing.)
CHILLI. This is real. The feelings I have for you, the feelings you are feeling for me, these are all real. Ive been fighting my feelings for years. With every dollar I made. Every hour I spent. I spent it fighting. Fighting my feelings. Maybe you did the same thing.

Maybe you remembered me against yr will, maybe you carried a torch for me against yr better judgment.

HESTER. You were my first.

CHILLI. Likewise.

(Rest.)

(He silently guesses the time and checks his guess against his watch. Is he right or wrong?)

"Yuck up my tragedy."

HESTER. Huh?

CHILLI. Marry me.

HESTER.

CHILLI.

HESTER. K.

CHILLI. There are some conditions some things we have to agree on. They dont have anything to do with money. I understand your situation.

HESTER. And my —

CHILLI. And your child — ok. *Our* child — ok. These things have to do with you and me. You would be mine and I would be yrs and all that. But I would still retain my rights to my manhood. You understand.

HESTER. Sure. My —

CHILLI. Yr kid. We'll get to him. I would rule the roost. I would call the shots. The whole roost and every single shot. Ive proven myself as a success. Youve not done that. It only makes sense that I would be in charge.

HESTER. — K.

CHILLI. Some people pile mistake upon mistake. You have just the one kid. Youve walked the line inspite of everything. And I respect you all the more for that.

HESTER. I love you.

CHILLI. Would you like me to get down on my knees?

(He gets down on his knees, offering her a ring.)

Heres an engagement ring. Its rather expensive. With an adjustable band. If I didnt find you I would have had to, well —. Try it on, try it on.

(Chilli checks his watch. As Hester fiddles with the ring, Bully &
Trouble rush in. Beauty & Baby follow them.)
BULLY. Mommie!
HESTER. No.
TROUBLE. You look fine!
HESTER. No.
BEAUTY. Is that a diamond?
HESTER. No!
BABY. Mommie!
(Hester recoils from her kids.)

HESTER.
BULLY/TROUBLE/BEAUTY/BABY.

BULLY. Mommie?
CHILLI. Who do we have here, honey?

HESTER.
BULLY/TROUBLE/BEAUTY/BABY.

CHILLI. Who do we have here?
HESTER. The neighbors kids.
(Chilli goes to look at his watch, doesnt.)
CHILLI. Honey?
HESTER. Bully, wheres Jabber at?
CHILLI. Honey?
HESTER. Bully, Im asking you a question.
CHILLI. Honey?
TROUBLE. He's out with Miga.
CHILLI. So you all are the neighbors kids, huh?
TROUBLE. Who the fuck are you?
HESTER. Trouble —
CHILLI. Who the fuck are you?
BULLY. We the neighbors kids.

CHILLI.
HESTER.

59

(Rest.)
CHILLI. Honey?
HESTER. Huh?
CHILLI. Im —. I'm thinking this through. I'm thinking this all the way through. And I think — I think —.
(Rest.)
(Rest.)
I carried around this picture of you. Sad and lonely with our child on yr hip. Stuggling to make do. Stuggling against all odds. And triumphant. Triumphant against everything. Like — hell, like Jesus and Mary. And if they could do it so could my Hester. My dear Hester. Or so I thought.
(Rest.)
But I dont think so.
(He takes her ring and her veil. He takes her dress. He packs up his basket.)
(Rest.)
HESTER. Please.
CHILLI. Im sorry.
(He looks at his watch, flipping it open and then snapping it shut. He leaves.)

Fifth Confession: Chilli
"We Was Young"

CHILLI.
We was young
and we didnt think
we didnt think that nothing we could do would hurt us
nothing we did would come back to haunt us
we was young and we knew all about gravity but gravity was a law
that did not apply to those persons under the age of 18
gravity was something that came later
and we was young and we could
float
weightless
I was her first

and zoom to the moon if we wanted and couldnt nothing stop us
We would go
fast
and we were gonna live forever
and any mistakes we would shake off
We were Death Defying
we were Hot Lunatics
careless as all get out
and she needed to keep it and I needed to leave town.
People get old that way.
(Rest.)
We didnt have a car and everything was pitched toward love in a car
and there was this car lot down from where we worked and
we were fearless
late nights go sneak in those rusted Buicks that hadnt moved in years
I would sit at the wheel and pretend to drive
and she would say she felt the wind in her face
surfing her hand out the window
Then we'd park
Without even moving
In the full light of the lot
Making love —
She was my first.
We was young.
Times change.

SCENE 8
THE HAND OF FATE

Night. The back entrance to the Reverends new church.
Hester comes in with the kids in tow.

HESTER. Sunday night. He had people in there listening to him
this morning. He passed the plate in my name. Not in my name
directly. Keeps me secret, cause, well, he has his image. I under-
stand that. Dont want to step on everything he's made for himself.
And he still wants me. I can tell. A woman can tell when a man
eyes her and he eyed me all right.
(Rest.)
Yr building this just from talking. Must be saying the right things.
Nobodyd ever give me nothing like this for running my mouth.
Gonna get me something now. Get something or do something.
Fuck you up fuck you up! Hold on, girl, it wont come to that.
(Rest.)
[I'll only ask for 5 dollars. 5 dollars a week. That way he cant say
no. And hes got a church, so he got 5 dollars. I'll say I need to buy
something for the kids. No. I'll say I need to — get my hair done.
There is this style, curls piled up on the head, I'll say. Takes hours
to do. I need to fix myself up, I'll say. Need to get my looks back.
Need to get my teeth done. Caps, bridges, what they called, fillers,
whatever. New teeth, dentures. Dentures. He dont cough up I'll
go straight to Welfare. Maybe.]
(Rest.)
(Jabber comes running around the building. He sees Hester and sneaks
up on her, touching her arm.)
JABBER. Yr it.
HESTER. I aint playing.
JABBER. K.
HESTER. Where you been.
JABBER. Out with Miga.

HESTER. Oh.
(Rest.)
JABBER. Mommie?
HESTER. What.

JABBER.
HESTER.

(Rest.)
JABBER. I dont like the moon.
HESTER. I'll cover it up for you. *(She holds her hand up in the sky, hiding the moon from view.)*
JABBER. Whered it go?
HESTER. Its gone to bed. You too.
(She nudges him away from her. He curls up with the others.)

HESTER.
HESTER.

(Reverend D. comes outside. He carries a large neon cross.)
HESTER. Its Sunday.
(He sees the children.)
REVEREND D. Oh God.
HESTER. Its Sunday. —. Yesterday was — Saturday.
REVEREND D. Excuse me a minute?
(He props the cross against a wall.)
HESTER. Its Sunday.
REVEREND D. I passed the plate and it came back empty.
HESTER. Oh.
REVEREND D. But not to worry: I'll have some. Tomorrow morning —
HESTER. I was gonna — get myself fixed up.
REVEREND D. — When the bank opens. 100 bucks. Tomorrow morning. All for you. You have my word.
HESTER. I was thinking, you know, in my head, that there was something I can do to stop that hand coming down. Must be something —
REVEREND D. I'll have my lawyer deliver the money. Its better

if you dont come back. Its too dangerous. My following are an angry bunch. They dont like the likes of you.

HESTER. But you do. You like me.

REVEREND D. Youd better go.

HESTER. Why you dont like me? Why you dont like me no more? *(He tries to go back inside. She grabs ahold of him.)*

HESTER. Dont go.

REVEREND D. Take yr hands off me.

HESTER. Why you dont like me?

(They struggle as he tries to shake her loose. Then, in a swift motion, she raises her club to strike him. He is much stronger than she. He brutally twists her hand. She recoils in pain and falls to the ground. Jabber, wide awake, watches.)

REVEREND D. Slut.

(Rest.)

Dont ever come back here again! Ever! Yll never get nothing from me! Common Slut. Tell on me! Go on! Tell the world! I'll crush you underfoot. *(He goes inside.)*

HESTER.
HESTER.
HESTER.

JABBER. Mommie.

HESTER.
HESTER.

JABBER. The moon came out again.

JABBER.
HESTER.
JABBER.

(Rest.)

JABBER. Them bad boys had writing. On our house. Remember the writing they had on our house and you told me to read it and I didnt wanna I said I couldnt but that wasnt really true I could I can read but I didnt wanna.

HESTER. Hush up now.

JABBER. I was reading it but I was only reading it in my head I wasnt reading it with my mouth I was reading it with my mouth but not with my tongue I was reading it only with my lips and I could hear the word outloud but only outloud in my head.

HESTER. Shhhh.

JABBER. I didnt wanna say the word outloud in your head.

HESTER.

HESTER.

JABBER. I didnt wanna say you the word. You wanna know why I didnt wanna say you the word? You wanna know why? Mommie?

HESTER.

HESTER.

(Rest.)

HESTER. What.

JABBER. It was a bad word.

HESTER.

HESTER.

JABBER. Wanna know what it was? Wanna know what the word was?

HESTER. What.

JABBER.

JABBER.

HESTER. What?

JABBER. "Slut."

HESTER. Go to sleep, Jabber.

JABBER. It read "Slut." "Slut."

HESTER. Hush up.

JABBER. Whassa "Slut"?

HESTER. Go sleep.

JABBER. You said if I read it youd say what it means. Slut. Whassit mean?

HESTER. I said I dont wanna hear that word. How slow are you? Slomo.

JABBER. Slut.

HESTER. You need to close yr mouth, Jabber.

JABBER. I know what it means. Slut.

HESTER. (Shut up.)

JABBER. Slut.

HESTER. (I said shut up, now.)

JABBER. I know what it means.

HESTER. (And I said shut up! Shut up.)

(Rest.)

(Rest.)

JABBER. Slut. Sorry.

(The word just popped out, a childs joke. He covers his mouth, sheepishly. They look at each other.)

HESTER.
JABBER.
HESTER.
JABBER.

(She quickly raises her club and hits him once. Brutally. He cries out and falls down dead. His cry wakes Bully, Trouble and Beauty. They look on. Hester beats Jabbers body again and again and again. Trouble and Bully back away. Beauty stands there watching. Jabber is dead and bloody. Hester looks up from her deed to see Beauty who runs off. Hester stands there alone — wet with her sons blood. Grief stricken, she cradles his body. Her hands wet with blood, she writes an A on ground.)

HESTER. Looks good, Jabber, dont it?

Dont it, huh?

Sixth Confession: Hester, La Negrita
"I Shoulda Had A Hundred-Thousand"

HESTER, LA NEGRITA.
Never shoulda had him.
Never shoulda had none of em.
Never was nothing but a pain to me:
5 Mistakes!
No, dont say that.
— nnnnnnnn —
Kids? Where you gone?
Never shoulda haddem.
Me walking around big as a house
Knocked up and Showing
and always by myself.
Men come near me oh yeah but then
love never sticks longer than a quick minute
wanna see something last forever watch water boil, you know.
I never shoulda haddem!
(Rest.)
(She places her hand in the pool of Jabbers blood.)
No:
I shoulda had a hundred
a hundred
I shoulda had a hundred-thousand
A hundred-thousand a whole *army* full I shoulda!
I shoulda.
One right after the other! Spitting em out with no years in
    between!
One after another:
Tail to head:
Spitting em out:
Bad mannered Bad mouthed Bad Bad *Bastards!*
A whole *army full* I shoulda!
I shoulda
— nnnnnnn —

I shoulda
(She sits there, crumpled, alone. The prison bars come down.)

SCENE 9
THE PRISON DOOR

All circle around Hester as they speak.

ALL.
LOOK AT HER!
WHO DOES SHE THINK
SHE IS
THE ANIMAL
NO SKILLS
CEPT ONE
CANT READ CANT WRITE
SHE MARRIED?
WHAT DO YOU THINK?
SHE OUGHTA BE MARRIED
SHE AINT MARRIED
THATS WHY THINGS ARE BAD LIKE THEY ARE
CAUSE OF
GIRLS LIKE THAT
THAT EVER HAPPEN TO ME YOU WOULDNT SEE ME
   DOING THAT
YOU WOULDNT SEE THAT HAPPENING TO ME
WHO THE HELL SHE THINK SHE IS
AND NOW SHES GOT TO PAY FOR IT
HAH!
(They spit.)
SHE DONT GOT NO SKILLS
CEPT ONE
CANT READ CANT WRITE
SHE MARRIED?

WHAT DO YOU THINK?
JUST PLAIN STUPID IF YOU ASK ME AINT NO SMART
WOMAN GOT ALL THEM BASTARDS
AND NOT A PENNY TO HER NAME
SOMETHINGS GOTTA BE DONE
CAUSE I'LL BE DAMNED IF SHE GONNA LIVE OFF ME

ALL.
HESTER.
ALL.

WELFARE. Is she in any pain?
DOCTOR. She shouldnt be. She wont be having anymore children.
WELFARE. No more mistakes.
CHILLI. Whats that?
WELFARE. An A.
AMIGA GRINGA. An A.
DOCTOR. First letter of the alphabet.
WELFARE. Thats as far as she got.
(Hester holds up her hands — theyre covered with blood. She looks up with outstretched arms.)
HESTER. Big hand coming down on me. Big hand coming down on me. Big hand coming down on me —

END OF PLAY

PROPERTY LIST

Soda cans (HESTER)
Ribbon (BEAUTY)
Bowls (TROUBLE)
Policeman's club (HESTER)
Soup pot, ladle (HESTER)
Shoebox with white pumps (HESTER)
Tape player, tape (HESTER)
Chalk (HESTER)
Eye-exam chart sandwich board (DOCTOR)
Vial of pills (DOCTOR)
$ (AMIGA GRINGA)
Box of matches (TROUBLE)
Framed picture of BABY (HESTER)
Doctor's shingle, black bag, instruments (DOCTOR)
Dolly (DOCTOR)
Flashlight (DOCTOR)
Toy cars (JABBER, TROUBLE, BEAUTY)
Comb (HESTER)
Pencil and paper (THE WELFARE LADY)
Cloth and sewing notions (THE WELFARE LADY)
Pocket watch (CHILLI)
Picnic basket with wedding dress (CHILLI)
Tape recorder with tape of "The Looking Song" (CHILLI)
Handkerchief (REVEREND D.)
Crumpled $ bill (REVEREND D.)
Large neon cross (REVEREND D.)
Tapes on sale (REVEREND D.)

SOUND EFFECTS

Reverend D.'s voice on tape
"The Looking Song" on tape

THE LOOKING SONG
Music and Lyrics by Suzan-Lori Parks

NEW PLAYS

★ **MOTHERS AND SONS by Terrence McNally.** At turns funny and powerful, MOTHERS AND SONS portrays a woman who pays an unexpected visit to the New York apartment of her late son's partner, who is now married to another man and has a young son. Challenged to face how society has changed around her, generations collide as she revisits the past and begins to see the life her son might have led. "A resonant elegy for a ravaged generation." –NY Times. "A moving reflection on a changed America." –Chicago Tribune. [2M, 1W, 1 boy] ISBN: 978-0-8222-3183-7

★ **THE HEIR APPARENT by David Ives, adapted from Le Légataire Universel by Jean-François Regnard.** Paris, 1708. Eraste, a worthy though penniless young man, is in love with the fair Isabelle, but her forbidding mother, Madame Argante, will only let the two marry if Eraste can show he will inherit the estate of his rich but miserly Uncle Geronte. Unfortunately, old Geronte has also fallen for the fair Isabelle, and plans to marry her this very day and leave her everything in his will—separating the two young lovers forever. Eraste's wily servant Crispin jumps in, getting a couple of meddling relatives disinherited by impersonating them (one, a brash American, the other a French female country cousin)—only to have the old man kick off before his will is made! In a brilliant stroke, Crispin then impersonates the old man, dictating a will favorable to his master (and Crispin himself, of course)—only to find that rich Uncle Geronte isn't dead at all and is more than ever ready to marry Isabelle! The multiple strands of the plot are unraveled to great comic effect in the streaming rhyming couplets of French classical comedy, and everyone lives happily, and richly, ever after. [4M, 3W] ISBN: 978-0-8222-2808-0

★ **HANDLE WITH CARE by Jason Odell Williams.** Circumstances both hilarious and tragic bring together a young Israeli woman, who has little command of English, and a young American man, who has little command of romance. Is their inevitable love an accident…or is it destiny, generations in the making? "A hilarious and heart-warming romantic comedy." –NY Times. "Hilariously funny! Utterly charming, fearlessly adorable and a tiny bit magical." –Naples News. [2M, 2W] ISBN: 978-0-8222-3138-7

★ **LAST GAS by John Cariani.** Nat Paradis is a Red Sox-loving part-time dad who manages Paradis' Last Convenient Store, the last convenient place to get gas—or anything—before the Canadian border to the north and the North Maine Woods to the west. When an old flame returns to town, Nat gets a chance to rekindle a romance he gave up on years ago. But sparks fly as he's forced to choose between new love and old. "Peppered with poignant characters [and] sharp writing." –Portland Phoenix. "Very funny and surprisingly thought-provoking." –Portland Press Herald. [4M, 3W] ISBN: 978-0-8222-3232-2

DRAMATISTS PLAY SERVICE, INC.
440 Park Avenue South, New York, NY 10016 212-683-8960 Fax 212-213-1539
postmaster@dramatists.com www.dramatists.com

NEW PLAYS

★ **ACT ONE by James Lapine.** Growing up in an impoverished Bronx family and forced to drop out of school at age thirteen, Moss Hart dreamed of joining the glamorous world of the theater. Hart's famous memoir *Act One* plots his unlikely collaboration with the legendary playwright George S. Kaufman and his arrival on Broadway. Tony Award-winning writer and director James Lapine has adapted Act One for the stage, creating a funny, heartbreaking and suspenseful celebration of a playwright and his work. "...brims contagiously with the ineffable, irrational and irrefutable passion for that endangered religion called the Theater." –NY Times. "...wrought with abundant skill and empathy." –Time Out. [8M, 4W] ISBN: 978-0-8222-3217-9

★ **THE VEIL by Conor McPherson.** May 1822, rural Ireland. The defrocked Reverend Berkeley arrives at the crumbling former glory of Mount Prospect House to accompany a young woman to England. Seventeen-year-old Hannah is to be married off to a marquis in order to resolve the debts of her mother's estate. However, compelled by the strange voices that haunt his beautiful young charge and a fascination with the psychic current that pervades the house, Berkeley proposes a séance, the consequences of which are catastrophic. "...an effective mixture of dark comedy and suspense." –Telegraph (London). "A cracking fireside tale of haunting and decay." –Times (London). [3M, 5W] ISBN: 978-0-8222-3313-8

★ **AN OCTOROON by Branden Jacobs-Jenkins. Winner of the 2014 OBIE Award for Best New American Play.** Judge Peyton is dead and his plantation Terrebonne is in financial ruins. Peyton's handsome nephew George arrives as heir apparent and quickly falls in love with Zoe, a beautiful octoroon. But the evil overseer M'Closky has other plans—for both Terrebonne and Zoe. In 1859, a famous Irishman wrote this play about slavery in America. Now an American tries to write his own. "AN OCTOROON invites us to laugh loudly and easily at how naïve the old stereotypes now seem, until nothing seems funny at all." –NY Times [10M, 5W] ISBN: 978-0-8222-3226-1

★ **IVANOV translated and adapted by Curt Columbus.** In this fascinating early work by Anton Chekhov, we see the union of humor and pathos that would become his trademark. A restless man, Nicholai Ivanov struggles to dig himself out of debt and out of provincial boredom. When the local doctor, Lvov, informs Ivanov that his wife Anna is dying and accuses him of worsening her condition with his foul moods, Ivanov is sent into a downward spiral of depression and ennui. He soon finds himself drawn to a beautiful young woman, Sasha, full of hope and energy. Finding himself stuck between a romantic young mistress and his ailing wife, Ivanov falls deeper into crisis, heading toward inevitable tragedy. [8M, 8W] ISBN: 978-0-8222-3155-4

DRAMATISTS PLAY SERVICE, INC.
440 Park Avenue South, New York, NY 10016 212-683-8960 Fax 212-213-1539
postmaster@dramatists.com www.dramatists.com

NEW PLAYS

★ **I'LL EAT YOU LAST: A CHAT WITH SUE MENGERS by John Logan.** For more than 20 years, Sue Mengers' clients were the biggest names in show business: Barbra Streisand, Faye Dunaway, Burt Reynolds, Ali MacGraw, Gene Hackman, Cher, Candice Bergen, Ryan O'Neal, Nick Nolte, Mike Nichols, Gore Vidal, Bob Fosse…If her clients were the talk of the town, she was the town, and her dinner parties were the envy of Hollywood. Now, you're invited into her glamorous Beverly Hills home for an evening of dish, dirty secrets and all the inside showbiz details only Sue can tell you. "A delectable soufflé of a solo show…thanks to the buoyant, witty writing of Mr. Logan" –NY Times. "80 irresistible minutes of primo tinseltown dish from a certified master chef." –Hollywood Reporter. [1W] ISBN: 978-0-8222-3079-3

★ **PUNK ROCK by Simon Stephens.** In a private school outside of Manchester, England, a group of highly-articulate seventeen-year-olds flirt and posture their way through the day while preparing for their A-Level mock exams. With hormones raging and minimal adult supervision, the students must prepare for their future — and survive the savagery of high school. Inspired by playwright Simon Stephens' own experiences as a teacher, PUNK ROCK is an honest and unnerving chronicle of contemporary adolescence. "[A] tender, ferocious and frightning play." –NY Times. "[A] muscular little play that starts out funny and ferocious then reveals its compassion by degrees." –Hollywood Reporter. [5M, 3W] ISBN: 978-0-8222-3288-9

★ **THE COUNTRY HOUSE by Donald Margulies.** A brood of famous and longing-to-be-famous creative artists have gathered at their summer home during the Williamstown Theatre Festival. When the weekend takes an unexpected turn, everyone is forced to improvise, inciting a series of simmering jealousies, romantic outbursts, and passionate soul-searching. Both witty and compelling, THE COUNTRY HOUSE provides a piercing look at a family of performers coming to terms with the roles they play in each other's lives. "A valentine to the artists of the stage." –NY Times. "Remarkably candid and funny." –Variety. [3M, 3W] ISBN: 978-0-8222-3274-2

★ **OUR LADY OF KIBEHO by Katori Hall.** Based on real events, OUR LADY OF KIBEHO is an exploration of faith, doubt, and the power and consequences of both. In 1981, a village girl in Rwanda claims to see the Virgin Mary. Ostracized by her schoolmates and labeled disturbed, everyone refuses to believe, until impossible happenings appear again and again. Skepticism gives way to fear, and then to belief, causing upheaval in the school community and beyond. "Transfixing." –NY Times. "Hall's passionate play renews belief in what theater can do." –Time Out [7M, 8W, 1 boy] ISBN: 978-0-8222-3301-5

DRAMATISTS PLAY SERVICE, INC.
440 Park Avenue South, New York, NY 10016 212-683-8960 Fax 212-213-1539
postmaster@dramatists.com www.dramatists.com

NEW PLAYS

★ **AGES OF THE MOON by Sam Shepard.** Byron and Ames are old friends, reunited by mutual desperation. Over bourbon on ice, they sit, reflect and bicker until fifty years of love, friendship and rivalry are put to the test at the barrel of a gun. "A poignant and honest continuation of themes that have always been present in the work of one of this country's most important dramatists, here reconsidered in the light and shadow of time passed." –NY Times. "Finely wrought…as enjoyable and enlightening as a night spent stargazing." –Talkin' Broadway. [2M] ISBN: 978-0-8222-2462-4

★ **ALL THE WAY by Robert Schenkkan. Winner of the 2014 Tony Award for Best Play.** November, 1963. An assassin's bullet catapults Lyndon Baines Johnson into the presidency. A Shakespearean figure of towering ambition and appetite, this charismatic, conflicted Texan hurls himself into the passage of the Civil Rights Act—a tinderbox issue emblematic of a divided America—even as he campaigns for re-election in his own right, and the recognition he so desperately wants. In Pulitzer Prize and Tony Award–winning Robert Schenkkan's vivid dramatization of LBJ's first year in office, means versus ends plays out on the precipice of modern America. ALL THE WAY is a searing, enthralling exploration of the morality of power. It's not personal, it's just politics. "…action-packed, thoroughly gripping… jaw-dropping political drama." –Variety. "A theatrical coup…nonstop action. The suspense of a first-class thriller." –NY1. [17M, 3W] ISBN: 978-0-8222-3181-3

★ **CHOIR BOY by Tarell Alvin McCraney.** The Charles R. Drew Prep School for Boys is dedicated to the creation of strong, ethical black men. Pharus wants nothing more than to take his rightful place as leader of the school's legendary gospel choir. Can he find his way inside the hallowed halls of this institution if he sings in his own key? "[An] affecting and honest portrait…of a gay youth tentatively beginning to find the courage to let the truth about himself become known." –NY Times. "In his stirring and stylishly told drama, Tarell Alvin McCraney cannily explores race and sexuality and the graces and gravity of history." –NY Daily News. [7M] ISBN: 978-0-8222-3116-5

★ **THE ELECTRIC BABY by Stefanie Zadravec.** When Helen causes a car accident that kills a young man, a group of fractured souls cross paths and connect around a mysterious dying baby who glows like the moon. Folk tales and folklore weave throughout this magical story of sad endings, strange beginnings and the unlikely people that get you from one place to the next. "The imperceptible magic that pervades human existence and the power of myth to assuage sorrow are invoked by the playwright as she entwines the lives of strangers in THE ELECTRIC BABY, a touching drama." –NY Times. "As dazzling as the dialogue is dreamful." –Pittsburgh City Paper. [3M, 3W] ISBN: 978-0-8222-3011-3

DRAMATISTS PLAY SERVICE, INC.
440 Park Avenue South, New York, NY 10016 212-683-8960 Fax 212-213-1539
postmaster@dramatists.com www.dramatists.com